ROYAL COURT

The Royal Court Theatre presents

A TIME TO REAP

by **Anna Wakulik**

translated by **Catherine Grosvenor**

A TIME TO REAP was first performed in this version at The Royal Court Jerwood Theatre Upstairs, Sloane Square, on Friday 22nd February 2013.

A TIME TO REAP is presented as part of International Playwrights: A Genesis Foundation Project

A TIME TO REAP

by **Anna Wakulik**

translated by **Catherine Grosvenor**

Cast in order of appearance
Marysia **Sinéad Matthews**
Piotr **Max Bennett**
Jan **Owen Teale**

Director **Caroline Steinbeis**
Designer **Max Jones**
Lighting Designer **Anna Watson**
Composer **Tom Mills**
Sound Designer **Alexander Caplen**
Casting Director **Amy Ball**
Assistant Director **Matt Steinberg**
Production Manager **Tariq Rifaat**
Stage Managers **Anna-Maria Casson & David Young**
Stage Management Work Placement **Alison Best**
Choreographer **Imogen Knight**
Costume Supervisor **Clare Wardroper**
Set Built by **Richard Martin**
Scenic Floor by **Footprint Scenery Ltd**

The Royal Court & Stage Management wish to thank the following for their help with this production:
William Drew, Ria Parry, Nic Wass, Jodi Gray, Apple Europe Ltd,
Dr. Richard Mole, Young Vic Theatre, National Theatre.

THE COMPANY

ANNA WAKULIK (Writer)

THEATRE INCLUDES: Zażynki [A Time to Reap], Sans Souci (Teatr Polski, Poznań); Elżbieta H. (Teatr Wybrzeże, Gdańsk); Krzywy Domek (Teatr Miejski, Gdynia); Bohaterowie (Teatr Solskiego, Tarnów).

AWARDS INCLUDE: Metaphors of Reality 2012 (Journalists' Prize); ASSITEJ Young Playwrights Award 2011.

Anna attended the Royal Court's International Residency for Emerging Playwrights 2011.

MAX BENNETT (Piotr)

FOR THE ROYAL COURT: Posh (Duke of York's), In Basildon.

THEATRE INCLUDES: The Promise (Donmar at Trafalgar Studios); Relatively Speaking (Theatre Royal Bath/Wyndham's); Luise Miller (Donmar); A Midsummer Night's Dream (Headlong); Fabrication [Affabulazione] (The Print Room); Danton's Death (National); Mrs Warren's Profession (Theatre Royal Bath/Comedy); Measure for Measure (Theatre Royal Plymouth/tour); Waste (Almeida); Romeo & Juliet (Theatre of Memory at Middle Temple Hall); Thyestes (BAC); Finisterre (503); The Herbal Bed (Salisbury Playhouse).

TELEVISION INCLUDES: Big Bad World.

FILM INCLUDES: Anna Karenina, The Numbers Station, The Sweeney, The Duchess, 99 Francs.

ALEXANDER CAPLEN (Sound Designer)

FOR THE ROYAL COURT: Ding Dong the Wicked, Goodbye to All That, Wanderlust, Over There (& Schaubühne, Berlin).

AS SOUND DESIGNER, OTHER THEATRE INCLUDES: Crave, Illusions, The Golden Dragon (ATC); Ogres (Tristan Bates); It's About Time (Nabokov); Mine, Ten Tiny Toes, War & Peace (Shared Experience); Stephen & the Sexy Partridge (Old Red Lion/Trafalgar Studios), Peter Pan, Holes, Duck Variations (UK tour); The Wizard of Oz, The Entertainer (Nuffield); Imogen (Ovalhouse/tour).

AS SOUND DESIGNER, OPERA INCLUDES: The Love for Three Oranges, Tosca (Grange Park Opera).

AS SOUND OPERATOR/ENGINEER, OTHER THEATRE INCLUDES: Edinburgh Military Tattoo 2009 - present; Brontë, Kindertransport (Shared Experience); Blood Brothers (International tour); Ballroom (UK tour). Other work includes large-scale music touring as a Front of House mix engineer. Alex is Sound Deputy at the Royal Court & an Associate Artist (Sound) for ATC.

CATHERINE GROSVENOR (Translator)

AS PLAYWRIGHT, THEATRE INCLUDES: Gabriel (Òran Mór); Cherry Blossom, One Day All This Will Come to Nothing (Traverse).

TRANSLATIONS & ADAPTATIONS INCLUDE: Continuous Growth by Esa Leskinen & Sami Keski-Vähälä, The Overcoat by Esa Leskinen & Sami Keski-Vähälä (Ryhmäteatteri/ACE Productions); The Amazon by Michał Walczak (Teatr Na Woli, Warsaw); dog where are we going by Anne Lepper (Berliner Festspiele).

LITERAL TRANSLATIONS INCLUDE: Our Class by Tadeusz Słobodzianek (National).

AWARDS INCLUDE: Scotsman Fringe First Award for Continuous Growth.

MAX JONES (Designer)

FOR THE ROYAL COURT: Spur of the Moment.

OTHER THEATRE INCLUDES: Glengarry Glen Ross, Bruised, A Doll's House, Dancing at Lughnasa, Blackthorn, A Small Family Business, Mary Stuart, Measure For Measure, Two Princes, The Grapes of Wrath (Theatre Clwyd); The Merry Wives of Windsor (RSC); Miss Julie (Royal Exchange, Manchester); Così Fan Tutte (Welsh National Opera/UK tour); Twist of Gold (Polka); A Day in the Life of Joe Egg, The Caretaker (Citizens'); Fatherland (Gate/ATC & Volkstheater, Munich); The Hard Man (King's, Edinburgh/UK Tour); Party (Arts); Mad Forest (BAC); Dumb Show (New Vic, Stoke); Sweeney Todd (Welsh National Youth Opera); The Life of Ryan & Ronnie (Script Cymru); Salt Meets Wound (503).

AWARDS INCLUDE: Linbury Biennial Prize for Stage Design.

Max is an Associate Artist at Theatre Clwyd.

SINÉAD MATTHEWS (Marysia)

THEATRE INCLUDES: The Changeling, The Glass Menagerie (Young Vic); The Way of the World, The Crucible (Sheffield Crucible); The Master & Margarita (Barbican/tour); Ecstasy (Hampstead/West End); Lulu (Gate/Headlong); Eigengrau, His Ghostly Heart/Little Dolls (Bush); Our Class, Women of Troy, The Mandate (National); The Wild Duck (Donmar); You Never Can Tell (Bath/tour/West End); The Birthday Party (West End); Spoonface Steinberg (Shaw).

TELEVISION INCLUDES: Way to Go, Black Mirror, Men are Wonderful, Half Broken Things, Ideal, Trial & Retribution, Who Gets the Dog, London, The Hogfather, Viva Las Blackpool, He Knew He Was Right.

FILM INCLUDES: Wreckers, Nanny McPhee & the Big Bang, Spring 1941, Happy Go Lucky, Pride & Prejudice, Vera Drake, Wednesday, Wraps.

RADIO INCLUDES: The Diary of a Nobody, A Girl in Winter, Mr Kipps.

TOM MILLS (Composer)

FOR THE ROYAL COURT: Wanderlust.

OTHER THEATRE INCLUDES: Titus Andronicus (RSC); Cesario, Prince of Denmark, The Eternal Not (National); Comedy of Errors (Cambridge Arts); Cinderella, Aladdin, Dick Whittington (Lyric Hammersmith); The Alchemist (Everyman Liverpool); The Boy Who Fell into a Book, Utopia, Mongrel Island, Realism (Soho); Boys, Clockwork, Dusk Rings A Bell (HighTide); Medea, A Midsummer Night's Dream, Edward Gant's Amazing Feats of Loneliness (Headlong); The Dark at the Top of the Stairs (Belgrade Coventry); The Littlest Quirky (UK tour); Benefactors, The Way of the World (Sheffield); Huis Clos, Lidless (Donmar/Trafalgar Studios); Great Expectations, Moonlight & Magnolias (Watermill); Purple Heart, Wittenburg, Electra, Breathing Irregular, The Kreutzer Sonata, Unbroken (Gate); Ahasverus (Hampstead); Pericles, Macbeth (Regent's Park); Oliver Twist, The Jungle Book (Bath); Elektra (Young Vic); Ditch (Old Vic Tunnels); The Grimm Brother's Circus, Metropolis (Theatre Royal Bath).

CAROLINE STEINBEIS (Director)

FOR THE ROYAL COURT: Royal Court Pussy Riot, Pereira's Bakery at 76 Chapel Road (New Plays from India Readings), Brilliant Adventures (Young Writers Festival Readings).

OTHER THEATRE INCLUDES: Earthquakes in London (Headlong UK tour); Fatherland (Gate/Radikal Jung Festival at the Volkstheater Munich); Charged/Re-Charged (Soho); Mad Forest, Photo Story (BAC); Mile End (Analogue).

OPERA INCLUDES: Cosi Fan Tutte (Sadler's Wells/Bridgewater Hall/Ascoli Festival).

AWARDS INCLUDE: The JMK Young Director's Award (Mad Forest).

Caroline is founder of Strike Ensemble. She is currently International Associate at the Royal Court.

MATT STEINBERG (Assistant Director)

AS DIRECTOR, THEATRE INCLUDES: Prime Targets (Toronto Fringe); Art & Scope (Tarragon).

AS ASSISTANT DIRECTOR, THEATRE INCLUDES: Romeo & Juliet (Canadian Stage Company).

AS PERFORMER, FILM INCLUDES: Kick Ass 2, Dirty Work, The Green Door.

AS PERFORMER, TELEVISION INCLUDES: The Best Years, Degrassi: The Next Generation, True Confessions of a Teenage Starlet, Trojan Horse.

AWARDS INCLUDE: Christopher Plummer Award (Shakespeare's Globe Centre of Canada); Tyrone Guthrie Award (Stratford Shakespeare Festival).

Matt has also worked as an actor with theatres including Finborough, Tristan Bates, Waterloo East, The Stratford Festival, Rattlestick, Classic Stage Company, Ensemble Studio, Threshold, HB Playwrights, Neptune, Tarragon, and the York Shakespeare Company.

OWEN TEALE (Jan)

FOR THE ROYAL COURT: The Country.

THEATRE INCLUDES: Anjin – The English Samurai (Tokyo); Mary Stuart, Macbeth (Clwyd); Creditors (Donmar/Brooklyn Academy); The Dance of Death (Lyric, West End/Sydney Festival); Ivanov, Berenice (National); A Doll's House (West End/Broadway); Love's Labour's Lost, The Merchant of Venice, King Lear, Julius Caesar, Henry IV Part I (RSC); The Comedy of Errors (Bristol Old Vic); When She Danced (King's Head); The Fifteen Streets (Belgrade Coventry/West End).

TELEVISION INCLUDES: Stella, Kidnap & Ransom, Game of Thrones, Silk, The Children, Lewis, Torchwood, Aftermath, Marian Again, Murphy's Law, Midsomer Murders, Murder in Rome, Spooks, Island at War, Ted & Alice, Judas & Jesus, Beast, Belonging, Ballykissangel, Love in the House of Our Lord, Wilderness, Death of a Salesman, The Thin Blue Line, Dangerous Lady, The Secret House of Death, The Vacillations of Poppy Carew, The Fifteen Streets, Great Expectations, Way Out of Order, David Copperfield.

FILM INCLUDES: Hunky Dory, Love Me Forever, Art in Las Vegas, The Last Legion, King Arthur, Conspiracy, Cleopatra, The Cherry Orchard, La Guerre des Moutons, Marco Polo, The Hawk, Robin Hood, War Requiem.

AWARDS INCLUDE: Tony Award for Best Featured Artist (A Doll's House).

ANNA WATSON (Lighting Designer)

THEATRE INCLUDES: Fireface, Disco Pigs, Sus (Young Vic); Salt, Root & Roe (Donmar at Trafalgar Studios); On the Record, It Felt Empty When the Heart Went At First But It Is Alright Now (Arcola); Eden End, In Praise of Love, The Talented Mr Ripley, My Zinc Bed (Northampton Royal); Paradise, Salt (Theatre Rites at The Ruhr Triennale, Germany); Gambling, This Wide Night (Soho); Plastic (Victoria Baths); Rutherford & Son, Ruby Moon (Northern Stage); King Pelican, Speed Death of the Radiant Child (Drum Theatre Plymouth); ... Sisters (Headlong/Gate).

OPERA INCLUDES: Orlando (Scottish Opera); Ruddigore (Opera North); Critical Mass (Almeida); Songs from a Hotel Bedroom, Tongue Tied (Linbury, ROH); The Bartered Bride (Royal College of Music).

DANCE INCLUDES: Refugees of a Septic Heart (The Garage); Soul Play (The Place); View from the Shore (Clore, ROH/Hall for Cornwall).

INTERNATIONAL PLAYWRIGHTS
AT THE ROYAL COURT THEATRE

Over the last two decades the Royal Court has led the way in the development and production of new international plays, facilitating work at grass roots level and developing exchanges which bring young writers and directors to work with emerging artists around the world. The International Department is the arm of the theatre dedicated to this work. Through a programme of long-term workshops and residencies, in London and abroad, a creative dialogue now exists with theatre practitioners from over 70 countries, working in over 30 languages, most recently Brazil, Chile, Cuba, Egypt, Georgia, India, Jordan, Lebanon, Mexico, Morocco, Nigeria, Palestine, Russia, Syria, Tunisia and Ukraine. All of these development projects are supported by the Genesis Foundation and the British Council.

The Royal Court has produced dozens of new international plays through this programme since 1997, most recently Remembrance Day by Aleksey Scherbak (Latvia) and Our Private Life by Pedro Miguel Rozo (Colombia) in 2011, Disconnect by Anupama Chandrasekhar (India) in 2010, The Stone by Marius von Mayenburg (Germany) in 2009 and Bliss by Olivier Choinière (Quebec) in 2008.

THE INTERNATIONAL RESIDENCY FOR EMERGING PLAYWRIGHTS

A Time to Reap was first developed on the Royal Court's 2011 International Residency for Emerging Playwrights. Anna Wakulik, aged 22, was the youngest of the ten international writers invited to participate. Since 1989 the Residency programme has offered hundreds of playwrights from around the world an opportunity to develop a new play with the Royal Court Theatre. At the same time it has provided international playwrights with a forum to meet and work with leading British writers, directors and performers. Almost all the international plays produced by the Royal Court have been by writers who have participated in this programme. These include the four international writers of the current Young Vic/Royal Court co-production of Feast; Yunior García Aguilera (Cuba), Rotimi Babatunde (Nigeria), Marcos Barbosa (Brazil) and Tanya Barfield (USA). Many past residency writers have gone on to become leading playwrights of their own countries. These include Marius von Mayenburg (Germany), Juan Mayorga (Spain), Rafael Spregelburd (Argentina), Anupama Chandrasekhar (India), Mikhail Durnenkov (Russia) and Natalia Vorozhbit (Ukraine).

After 24 years, the International Residency remains a springboard for new international playwrights around the world.

The Genesis Foundation supports the Royal Court's International Playwrights Programme. To find and develop the next generation of professional playwrights, the Genesis Foundation funds workshops in diverse countries as well as residencies at the Royal Court. The Foundation's involvement extends to productions and rehearsed readings which helps the Royal Court to provide a springboard for young writers to greater public and critical attention. For more information, please visit www.genesisfoundation.org.uk.

A TIME TO REAP is presented as part of International Playwrights: A Genesis Foundation Project and produced by the Royal Court's International Department:

Associate Director International **Elyse Dodgson**
International Projects Manager **Chris James**
International Associate **Caroline Steinbeis**

THE ENGLISH STAGE COMPANY
AT THE ROYAL COURT THEATRE

'For me the theatre is really a religion or way of life. You must decide what you feel the world is about and what you want to say about it, so that everything in the theatre you work in is saying the same thing ... A theatre must have a recognisable attitude. It will have one, whether you like it or not.'

George Devine, first artistic director of the English Stage Company: notes for an unwritten book.

photo: Stephen Cummiskey

As Britain's leading national company dedicated to new work, the Royal Court Theatre produces new plays of the highest quality, working with writers from all backgrounds, and addressing the problems and possibilities of our time.

"The Royal Court has been at the centre of British cultural life for the past 50 years, an engine room for new writing and constantly transforming the theatrical culture." Stephen Daldry

Since its foundation in 1956, the Royal Court has presented premieres by almost every leading contemporary British playwright, from John Osborne's Look Back in Anger to Caryl Churchill's A Number and Tom Stoppard's Rock 'n' Roll. Just some of the other writers to have chosen the Royal Court to premiere their work include Edward Albee, John Arden, Richard Bean, Samuel Beckett, Edward Bond, Leo Butler, Jez Butterworth, Martin Crimp, Ariel Dorfman, Stella Feehily, Christopher Hampton, David Hare, Eugène Ionesco, Ann Jellicoe, Terry Johnson, Sarah Kane, David Mamet, Martin McDonagh, Conor McPherson, Joe Penhall, Lucy Prebble, Mark Ravenhill, Simon Stephens, Wole Soyinka, Polly Stenham, David Storey, Debbie Tucker Green, Arnold Wesker and Roy Williams.

"It is risky to miss a production there." Financial Times

In addition to its full-scale productions, the Royal Court also facilitates international work at a grass roots level, developing exchanges which bring young writers to Britain and sending British writers, actors and directors to work with artists around the world. The research and play development arm of the Royal Court Theatre, The Studio, finds the most exciting and diverse range of new voices in the UK. The Studio runs play-writing groups including the Young Writers Programme, Critical Mass for black, Asian and minority ethnic writers and the biennial Young Writers Festival. For further information, go to www.royalcourttheatre.com/playwriting/the-studio.

"Yes, the Royal Court is on a roll. Yes, Dominic Cooke has just the genius and kick that this venue needs... It's fist-bitingly exciting." Independent

Spring 2013

Jerwood Theatre Downstairs

15 Feb–9 Mar 2013

if you don't let us dream, we won't let you sleep
by Anders Lustgarten

A new play exploring the ethos of austerity and offering an alternative.

Part of the Royal Court's Jerwood New Playwrights programme,
Supported by the Jerwood Charitable Foundation

21 Mar–11 May 2013

the low road
by Bruce Norris

A fable of free market economics and cut-throat capitalism.
Bruce Norris' previous plays include *Clybourne Park* at the Royal Court.

Jerwood Theatre Upstairs

5 Apr–4 May 2013

a new play
by Anthony Neilson

Neilson is renowned for his ground-breaking and imaginative new work.

11 May–8 Jun 2013
Royal Court Theatre and Fuel co-production

the victorian in the wall
by Will Adamsdale

Perrier Award winner Adamsdale's new play contains jokes, songs,
banging on recycling boxes, a talking fridge…

020 7565 5000
www.royalcourttheatre.com

⊖ Sloane Square ⇌ Victoria ⏺ royalcourt ⏹ theroyalcourttheatre

Principal Sponsor **Coutts**

Supported using public funding by
**ARTS COUNCIL
ENGLAND**

ROYAL COURT SUPPORTERS

The Royal Court has significant and longstanding relationships with many organisations and individuals who provide vital support. It is this support that makes possible its unique playwriting and audience development programmes.

Coutts is the Principal Sponsor of the Royal Court. The Genesis Foundation supports the Royal Court's work with International Playwrights. Theatre Local is sponsored by Bloomberg. The Jerwood Charitable Foundation supports new plays by playwrights through the Jerwood New Playwrights series. The Andrew Lloyd Webber Foundation supports the Royal Court's Studio, which aims to seek out, nurture and support emerging playwrights.

The Harold Pinter Playwright's Award is given annually by his widow, Lady Antonia Fraser, to support a new commission at the Royal Court.

PUBLIC FUNDING
Arts Council England, London
British Council
European Commission Representation in the UK

CHARITABLE DONATIONS
Martin Bowley Charitable Trust
Columbia Foundation Fund of the London Community Foundation
Cowley Charitable Trust
The Dorset Foundation
The John Ellerman Foundation
The Eranda Foundation
Genesis Foundation
J Paul Getty Jnr Charitable Trust
The Golden Bottle Trust
The Haberdashers' Company
Jerwood Charitable Foundation
Marina Kleinwort Trust
The Andrew Lloyd Webber Foundation
John Lyon's Charity
The Andrew W. Mellon Foundation
Rose Foundation
The Royal College of Psychiatrists
Royal Victoria Hall Foundation
The Dr Mortimer & Theresa Sackler Foundation
John Thaw Foundation
The Vandervell Foundation
The Garfield Weston Foundation

CORPORATE SUPPORTERS & SPONSORS
BBC
Bloomberg
Cream
Coutts
Ecosse Films
Kudos Film & Television
MAC
Moët & Chandon
Oakley Capital Limited
Smythson of Bond Street
White Light Ltd

BUSINESS ASSOCIATES, MEMBERS & BENEFACTORS
Annoushka
Auerbach & Steele Opticians
Bank of America Merrill Lynch
Byfield Consultancy
Hugo Boss
Lazard
Savills
Troy Asset Management
Vanity Fair

DEVELOPMENT ADVOCATES
John Ayton MBE
Elizabeth Bandeen
Kinvara Balfour
Anthony Burton CBE
Piers Butler
Sindy Caplan
Sarah Chappatte
Cas Donald (Vice Chair)
Celeste Fenichel
Emma Marsh (Chair)
Deborah Shaw Marquardt (Vice Chair)
Tom Siebens
Sian Westerman
Daniel Winterfeldt

Principal Sponsor

Supported by
ARTS COUNCIL ENGLAND

INDIVIDUAL MEMBERS

GROUND-BREAKERS

Anonymous
Moira Andreae
Allen Appen & Jane Wiest
Mr & Mrs Simon Andrews
Nick Archdale
Charlotte Asprey
Jane Attias
Brian Balfour-Oatts
Elizabeth & Adam Bandeen
Ray Barrell & Ursula Van Almsick
Dr Kate Best
Sarah & David Blomfield
Stan & Val Bond
Kristina Borsy & Nick Turdean
Neil & Sarah Brener
Deborah Brett
Mrs Joanna Buckhenham
Lois Moore & Nigel Burridge
Louise Burton
Clive & Helena Butler
Sindy & Jonathan Caplan
Gavin & Lesley Casey
Sarah & Philippe Chappatte
Tim & Caroline Clark
Carole & Neville Conrad
Anthony & Andrea Coombs
Clyde Cooper
Ian & Caroline Cormack
Mr & Mrs Cross
Andrew & Amanda Cryer
Alison Davies
Matthew Dean
Roger & Alison De Haan
Noel De Keyzer
Polly Devlin OBE
Sophie Diedrichs-Cox
Glen Donovan
Denise & Randolph Dumas
Robyn Durie
Zeina Durra & Saadi Soudavar
Glenn & Phyllida Earle

The Edwin Fox Foundation
Lisa Erikson & Edward Ocampo
Mark & Sarah Evans
Celeste & Peter Fenichel
Deborah Ferreira
Beverley Gee
Nick & Julie Gould
Lord & Lady Grabiner
Richard & Marcia Grand
Reade & Elizabeth Griffith
Don & Sue Guiney
Jill Hackel & Andrzej Zarzycki
Carol Hall
Jennifer & Stephen Harper
Sam & Caroline Haubold
Madeleine Hodgkin
Mr & Mrs Gordon Holmes
Damien Hyland
Susie & David Hyman
Amanda Ibbetson
Nicholas Jones
David Kaskel & Christopher Teano
Vincent & Amanda Keaveny
Peter & Maria Kellner
Nicola Kerr
Mr & Mrs Pawel Kisielewski
Sarah & David Kowitz
Rosemary Leith
Larry & Peggy Levy
Imelda Liddiard
Daisy & Richard Littler
Kathryn Ludlow
Beatrice & James Lupton CBE
Dr Ekaterina Malievskaia & George Goldsmith
Christopher Marek Rencki
Andy McIver
Barbara Minto
Shafin & Angelie Moledina
Ann & Gavin Neath CBE

Clive & Annie Norton
Georgia Oetker
James Orme-Smith
Mr & Mrs Sandy Orr
Mr & Mrs Guy Patterson
Sir William & Lady Vanessa Patey
William Plapinger & Cassie Murray
Andrea & Hilary Ponti
Lauren Prakke
Annie & Preben Prebensen
Mrs Ivetta Rabinovich
Julie Ritter
Mark & Tricia Robinson
Paul & Gill Robinson
Corinne Rooney
Sir & Lady Ruddock
William & Hilary Russell
Julie & Bill Ryan
Sally & Anthony Salz
Bhags Sharma
J Sheridan
The Michael & Melanie Sherwood Charitable Foundation
Tom Siebens & Mimi Parsons
Andy Simpkin
Anthony Simpson & Susan Boster
Andrea Sinclair & Serge Kremer
Paul & Rita Skinner
Mr & Mrs RAH Smart
Brian Smith
Sue St Johns
The Ulrich Family
The Ury Trust
Amanda Vail
Constanze Von Unruh
Ian & Victoria Watson & The Watson Foundation
Matthew & Sian Westerman
Anne-Marie Williams
Sir Robert & Lady Wilson
Daniel Winterfeldt & Jonathan Leonhart
Martin & Sally Woodcock
Kate & Michael Yates

BOUNDARY-BREAKERS

Anonymous

Katie Bradford
David Harding
Steve Kingshott
Philip & Joan Kingsley
Emma Marsh
Philippa Thorp
Mr & Mrs Nick Wheeler

MOVER-SHAKERS

Eric Abraham
Anonymous
Christine Collins
Piers & Melanie Gibson
Lydia & Manfred Gorvy
Mr & Mrs Roderick Jack
Duncan Matthews QC
Ian & Carol Sellars
Edgar & Judith Wallner

MAJOR DONORS

Anonymous
Rob & Siri Cope
Cas Donald
Jack & Linda Keenan
Adam Kenwright
Miles Morland
NoraLee & Jon Sedmak
Jan & Michael Topham
Stuart & Hilary Williams Charitable Foundation

Thank you to all our Friends, Stage-Takers and Ice-Breakers for their generous support.

APPLAUDING
THE EXCEPTIONAL.

Coutts is proud to sponsor the Royal Court Theatre

Coutts ♚

A TIME TO REAP

Anna Wakulik

Translated by Catherine Grosvenor

Characters

MARYSIA, *twenty-five*

JAN, *fifty*

PIOTR, *twenty-five*

Note on the Text

The play jumps in place and time. We are taken through the various locations by the actors. Scenes play in Niepokalanów, Warsaw and London.

Our key date is 15th August, the Feast of the Assumption of the Virgin Mary. The scene is rural and centred around the local church in Niepokalanów.

The actors are on stage throughout the play. They observe each other. We are in a theatre. There is no pretence of a fourth wall.

This text went to press before the end of rehearsals and so may differ slightly from the play as performed.

Scene One – Prologue

MARYSIA. I'm four years old. This boy – (*Points at* PIOTR.) comes to our town of Niepokalanów for the festival. The boy's called Piotruś. He can't pronounce his 'r's, which I think is funny and also iwwitating.

PIOTR. I'm four years old – today. I don't like girls. We came here on the train today, me and Mummy and Daddy. Bye-bye Warsaw, we'll be back soon, Daddy just has to go back to the sticks and visit his mummy!

MARYSIA. He's funny, this boy. He's got a Tamagotchi. A real one. And these trainers that light up when he walks. I think they're the coolest things I've ever seen in my life.

JAN. It's 1989. I'm twenty-nine years old. Things are all right. I've planted a child, fathered a house and built a tree. I don't like it when people are late, I'm one of the most successful gynaecologists in Warsaw, I have my own practice, I go jogging, I don't believe in God, I believe in what's in front of me.

PIOTR. It's August the fifteenth, the day when the Virgin Mary was assumed into Heaven. But really, it's my birthday.

MARYSIA. Mummy's working today, making lots and lots of flowers for church. Our church is special. The Pope came to bless it once because a real Saint lived in Niepokalanów and that makes our town the holiest in all of Poland. Daddy's got the day off, because he doesn't have to deliver letters on Sundays.

Hi, Piotruś.

JAN. Don't be shy, Piotruś.

PIOTR. Hi, Marysia.

MARYSIA. Do you want to play?

PIOTR. Let's play doctors and nurses.

MARYSIA. How do you play that?

PIOTR. First you have to kiss me.

MARYSIA. Yuck.

PIOTR. I've brushed my teeth.

MARYSIA. But you've got all saliva in your mouth.

PIOTR. All right then. I'll find another friend. See you.

MARYSIA. No, wait. I'll do it.

They kiss incompetently.

JAN. What are you two doing? What kind of games do kids
   play around here? Playtime's over! Piotrek, go in and see
   your granny. Then she might stop complaining that she never
   gets to see you.

PIOTR. I don't want to! She's ugly and stupid.

JAN. I think the same thing myself sometimes, but luckily I
   only need to see her three times a year: Christmas, Easter
   and Assumption Day. I come with all the other pilgrims. That
   keeps her happy.

PIOTR. Granny shouts at me cos I don't know that rhyme.
   Marysia, you're pretty, you practise with me.

MARYSIA. What rhyme?

PIOTR. About being Polish.

MARYSIA. The catechism? Everyone knows that!

PIOTR. It's silly.

MARYSIA. Aren't you proud to be Polish?

PIOTR. I don't know.

MARYSIA. I thought people from Warsaw knew everything.

PIOTR. If you practise with me, you can play with my
   Tamagotchi.

MARYSIA. Who are you?

   PIOTR *can't remember how the rhyme goes.*

PIOTR. – I'm a Pole, young and bright.

MARYSIA. What's your sign?

PIOTR. – The eagle white.

MARYSIA. Good. Where do you live?

PIOTR. In Warsaw! And I wished you lived there too.

MARYSIA. On Polish soil. What will you do for her?

PIOTR. – I will sweat and toil.

MARYSIA. What is this place?

PIOTR. – My motherland dear.

MARYSIA. How was she gained?

PIOTR. – With blood and tears.

MARYSIA. Do you love her?

PIOTR. – With all my heart.

MARYSIA. What do you believe in?

PIOTR. – In Poland, every part.

MARYSIA. Will you defend her?

PIOTR. – With sword and knife!

MARYSIA. What will you give her? (*Beat.*) I'll give her my life!

   I'm eight years old. Mum says that from today people won't
   be able to kill babies in their mummies' tummies any more.
   It's a sin and finally it's going to be banned. I say that I
   would never do something like that, never ever.

JAN. January 1993. The anti-abortion bill is signed, because we
   live in a Catholic country. The Pope says: 'I forbid it!' He
   wants things in Europe to be the same as they are in Africa.
   I'm thirty-three. The same age as Christ. My life has never
   been so good, and it's only going to get better.

PIOTR. Wow, Dad, a bike! It's amazing! Thanks! I love you, I love you this much!

JAN. Thank you, Catholic Church, who thanks to my parents I have hated with all my heart from dusk till dawn. I have hated you poetically, I have hated you with swirls and curls and glorious fanfares, but now I thank you. I thank you for signing this wonderful contract with our nation! Thank you for protecting our unborn, unwanted children. Thanks to you, I suddenly become one of the most sought-after gynaecologists in Warsaw. Thanks to you, I now start to earn decent money.

PIOTR. Money?

JAN. Sometimes there are days where I have two procedures after hours. Each one costs the patient the best part of her month's salary. My wife –

PIOTR. Mummy?

JAN. – pretends that she doesn't know anything. But when we move out of our block of flats into a house with a garden and a hammock and a veranda – she still doesn't ask. She doesn't ask me much any more.

PIOTR. February 1993. I saw Daddy crying for the first time today, in the toilet. I don't know why.

JAN. There are only complications once. The patient dies. She's a friend of my wife's. Fortunately, she had underlying health issues. I write that on her record. 'Spontaneous miscarriage, haemorrhage.' I don't cry, I can deal with it. But I'm so scared I piss my pants, even though I know that there won't be an investigation. No one will check, no one will sue. They put her in a bag and take her away. I disinfect the surgery for six hours. I do everything, including my cotton-wool buds and my toothbrush. That night my wife leaves me.

PIOTR. 1997. I'm twelve years old. I smoked a cigarette today. Dad didn't notice.

JAN. My son smoked a cigarette today. He thinks I didn't notice. I'm thirty-seven, I'm a professional, no distinguishing features.

MARYSIA. I'm twelve years old and I'm a child. I go to confession because I'm wearing a bra for the first time and I think I'm immorally dressed.

PIOTR. I'm fifteen years old. I go swimming twice a week and to English lessons three times a week. I enjoy reading good literature.

PIOTR *pulls out a copy of* Playboy. *He hides it inside his school atlas.*

JAN. What are you doing?

PIOTR. I'm reading.

JAN. For school?

PIOTR. For school.

JAN. Have you got a lot to go?

PIOTR. Another hundred pages or so.

JAN. Keep at it. Education is your ticket to success!

MARYSIA. I'm fifteen years old and I'm a child.

JAN. 2002. The Millennium Bridge opens in London. A Polish skier wins silver for the first time in thirty years at the Winter Olympics in Salt Lake City. I'm forty-two years old.

MARYSIA. I'm seventeen years old and I'm a woman.

PIOTR. I'm seventeen years old. Dad wants me to be a lawyer. I want to be a film director.

MARYSIA. I'm a woman now. There's no doubt about it any more.

PIOTR. 2007. Warsaw is a boring, post-Communist shithole. I apply to do my Masters in London.

JAN (*holding an envelope*). 'Mr Piotr'…? 'Mr Piotr'? I don't think anyone by that name lives here.

PIOTR. What's that?

JAN. I don't know. It says it's from the London School of Economics. Hmmm. They must have sent it to me by accident.

PIOTR. Is it a thick envelope or a thin one? If it's thin, they're just writing to say thanks but no thanks. Tell me it's thick!

JAN. Well… It's hard to say… I suppose I'd have to say it's really quite… THICK!

PIOTR. Sixteen of their alumni have won the Nobel Prize! I'm going to be walking along the same corridors as they did!

JAN. I should be having one of those mid-life crises. Get myself a better car, or a young girlfriend. I don't have a new car. Or a girlfriend. That stuff's for idiots.

MARYSIA. You never know what tomorrow will bring.

PIOTR. I'm twenty-five.

MARYSIA. I'm twenty-five.

JAN. I'm fifty.

ALL. I'm going back to Niepokalanów for the day.

JAN. I suggest it, to celebrate my son's birthday. It was very clever of him to be born on Assumption Day. It's always a glorious day. The height of summer. The entire country takes the day off and celebrates with him. Beers in the fridge, sausages on the barbecue. It's like a ready-made party. Unfortunately, I also have to endure the church procession, the endless songs about the Virgin Mary and the tat they sell at the village fair. But I'd do anything for my son.

MARYSIA. If you want to go, go. I've got too much work to do.

JAN. Don't you want to come with me?

A look.

PIOTR. I've come from London. I said yes straight away. I had a shot of vodka on the plane. I'd been wanting to go and visit him anyway. I'm homesick.

JAN. Of course he says yes. The tone of his voice said: 'I'm in trouble!' But it doesn't matter. I like him. He's my son. I had a little drink this morning. You're all right to drive if you've just had the one.

MARYSIA. I've come from Warsaw. With my… boss.

JAN. I've come from Warsaw. With my… assistant.

MARYSIA. Today is a day when Polish coins will mingle with British ones. When the past will merge with the present.

Today is a day of endings and beginnings, of sowing and reaping. God, please help me. I have sinned. Come and show yourself to me. Be wise and shining, just like you were when I was a child.

A bell strikes noon.

PIOTR *and* JAN. 'Then the sanctuary of God in Heaven opened, and the Ark of the Covenant could be seen inside it. Now a great sign appeared in Heaven: a woman, robed with the Sun, standing on the Moon, and on her head a crown of twelve stars. Then a second sign appeared in the sky: there was a huge red dragon with seven heads and ten horns, and each of the seven heads crowned with a coronet. Its tail swept a third of the stars from the sky and hurled them to the ground, and the dragon stopped in front of the woman as she was at the point of giving birth, so that it could eat the child as soon as it was born.'

Scene Two

15th August 2010. Niepokalanów. Outside the church.

JAN *and* MARYSIA *are playing Taboo.*

JAN (*with a card in his hand*). This is you.

MARYSIA. Woman.

JAN. Smaller.

MARYSIA. Girl.

JAN. In general. My – Piotr.

MARYSIA. Child.

JAN (*satisfied, taking the next card*). This circulates.

MARYSIA. Gossip.

JAN. Physically.

MARYSIA. Air.

JAN. In you.

MARYSIA. Blood.

JAN (*pleased that she's got it*). Man creates him and then thinks he created man.

MARYSIA. I don't know.

JAN. Yes you do. Come on.

MARYSIA. I don't know.

JAN. This is the last one.

MARYSIA. I don't know.

JAN. Have a guess and we'll stop playing.

MARYSIA. God.

>JAN *nods and smiles.*

>Do you think he's going to be pleased to get a game of Taboo for his twenty-fifth birthday?

JAN. What are you talking about? It's a fantastic game! I think it's the best there is. It develops the brain cells.

>*They are at the entrance to the church.*

MARYSIA. Are you going to come in?

JAN. No.

MARYSIA. Grit your teeth and come in. Just once. What's the worst that can happen?

>*They walk into the church.* MARYSIA *crosses herself with holy water.*

>I've always loved hiding inside a cool church in the middle of summer.

>JAN *starts to eat an apple.*

What are you doing? You can't eat in here!

JAN. 'Not that which goeth into the mouth defileth a man; but that which cometh out of the mouth, this defileth a man.'

MARYSIA. Look at these flowers. They're so beautiful. I wonder if it was my mum who did them. It might have been her who did the flowers for your wedding, you know.

JAN. I'm allergic to incense and I've got a sore throat. It's too cold in here. I'm going to go back over to the fair, buy some more crap and do some people-watching. It's like time has stood still for this lot. Anyone would think they didn't have electricity round here. They look like they're praying for rain.

MARYSIA. I'm sure they'll welcome their beloved doctor back with open arms. Just the way you like it. Will you buy me some sweets?

JAN. With your teeth in the state they're in? You'll regret it.

MARYSIA. Things would be a lot easier between us if you were a dentist.

JAN. Let's not talk about work today. At work, I'm professional. I'm Dr House. Here, I'm off-duty.

MARYSIA. Go on, get out of here, Doubting Thomas, I'm going to go to confession.

JAN. You never go in Warsaw. Despite your protestations of piety. What are you going to confess now?

MARYSIA. You. You should go too.

JAN. There's no point. Our friend up there gave up on me a long time ago. I was waiting in the queue for surgical talent and it took so long I never made it to the queue for morality. I'm one of the bad guys.

MARYSIA. That's not true. You're the most sensitive person I know.

JAN. Me? Sensitive?

MARYSIA. In here – (*Points at his ribcage.*) I saw you when you hit that fox on the road today.

JAN. What fox?

MARYSIA. Its guts were all over the road and you started crying.

JAN. That's not true.

MARYSIA. I'm going to confession. (*Motions at him to go away.*)

JAN. There's no priest.

MARYSIA. You can confess alone. I had a dream about these little kittens. They were soaking wet. They'd been abandoned. And then this yellow flower grew out of my stomach and exploded.

JAN. You might have a magnesium deficiency. You should take more vitamins.

MARYSIA. Then I dreamed that I had to pay you if I wanted to touch you.

JAN (*as though he were explaining something to a child*). When you dream, you're grinding up your day. Your day is a chunk of meat and your dreams are hamburgers. Do you know what I mean? But it's all made from that original chunk of meat. What you see in your head at night are puzzles left over from your day. Well. This is probably a good moment for me to leave you in your dark medieval world and get back into the heat. May the Father, the Son and the Holy Ghost be with you, amen.

JAN *throws his apple core onto the ground, but then picks it up and exits.*

Scene Three

15th August 2010. Niepokalanów. In the church.

Confession.

MARYSIA. 'Being with child and in labour, I cry out, travailing in birth and in pain to be delivered': Bless me, Father, for I have sinned. It has been seven years since my last confession. I did my penance but then I offended God with my subsequent sins.

I'm seventeen years old. I'm at my church's summer camp, the same one I go to every year. It's so hot this summer that the butter melts and falls off my knife before I can get it onto my bread.

There are children everywhere. Sweaty trainers. Lingering fifteen-year-old gazes. Crickets chirp in the heat. The mosquitoes have already eaten half my body. I've got red patches on my sunburned skin.

This is my last holiday camp. The seventh day.

On the seventh day, God had had enough and he sat down for a rest. The church belches out the accumulated heat of the day. A stream of sweat runs down my spine.

He's sweating under his cassock too. 'You're a very interesting person, and very mature for your age.' It's the first time anyone's ever said anything like that to me and suddenly I can feel that I'm growing breasts and earrings and high heels and painted nails. I walk behind him on purpose. I leave him little letters. I draw hearts on the door to his room. I put my hand up when he asks us what we know about the Pharisee and the sinful woman. I learn all the prayers off by heart. I read the Bible at night so I'll have a new quote for him in the morning.

He's been sitting in his black cassock for a week. Does he have spare ones? Does he wash them at night? Isn't he hot?

'If you're not sure, then go. But if you're sure – then don't be afraid.'

He wasn't drunk. A glass of wine. Him and me. I wanted to.

Love is not what you feel, it's what you decide to do, our Polish Pope said. I decided.

I wore my ripped blouse with pride for a whole month. I kissed the bruise on my forearm until it faded. That was the first time I knew what it meant to bleed. The first time I felt that fear. The first time I realised that you can do something which can't be undone. I am sorry for these and all the sins of my past life. The heat. The heat. The heat.

The bell and the sound of mosquitoes and a meadow at the end of summer, growing louder.

Scene Four

October 2002. Warsaw. JAN*'s surgery.*

JAN. Hot today, isn't it?

MARYSIA. Jan said, when I met him that summer, seven years ago in Warsaw.

JAN. Actually, it was already winter.

MARYSIA. It was early autumn. And the summer had been really good that year.

JAN. I was surprised to see her.

MARYSIA. I'd never seen a doctor's surgery like it in my life. In Niepokalanów, it's all crumbling plaster and peeling paint, and look at this – all glass and plastic. Very nice.

JAN. I wanted to help her.

MARYSIA. I'm not embarrassed. I'll never have to see him again if I don't want to. I wondered if you might be able to help me, doctor.

JAN. Help you?

MARYSIA. That's how I asked him. I felt so stupid. You're the only person I know here. All I have is what I'm standing up in.

JAN. You're all grown up. You were a lot smaller last time I saw you.

MARYSIA. And you hadn't gone grey, doctor, and your car had Warsaw licence plates and everyone was jealous.

JAN. What month are you?

MARYSIA. Second. And a half. Third, in fact. I don't have any money. Nothing. Zero.

JAN. Are you sure this is what you want to do?

MARYSIA. One million billion per cent.

JAN. And the father? Who's the father?

MARYSIA. The Holy Spirit.

JAN. How's your mum?

MARYSIA. My mum? She says I should get a job, and there are more opportunities in Warsaw, a whole load of opportunities! But you need a degree to get any job in this city. I don't stand a chance. What am I meant to do, become a cleaner? No thanks. Or be a waitress? That's not a proper job either. I'm going to apply to uni next year. I'm going to study architecture and be an architect.

JAN. Can you use Microsoft Office?

MARYSIA. No. But I can learn.

JAN. Excel?

MARYSIA. No. But I can learn.

JAN. Invoicing?

MARYSIA. No. But I can learn.

JAN. How's your English?

MARYSIA. It's all right. Improving.

JAN. It's a very simple medical procedure.

MARYSIA. Mum says it's murder.

JAN. The womb is cleaned out by a process called dilation and evacuation. The patient is under anaesthetic and you can usually go home the same day.

MARYSIA. I don't have a home any more.

JAN. Come back tomorrow. I'll be waiting for you.

MARYSIA. All night long I lie there and imagine my tummy getting bigger and bigger. As it grows, I can feel my dreams being rubbed out one by one. I know that soon there won't be any time for anything, that I'll let myself go, and I'll be like my mother, that the baby will put the brakes on my life, just like she always told me it would. I remember everything about that day.

JAN. I don't really remember that day. It was like all the others. Monday or Tuesday.

MARYSIA. It was Friday, the first Friday of the month. If I'd been back home in Niepokalanów, I'd have been going to confession with everyone else.

JAN. Gown. Mask. Latex gloves.

MARYSIA. Warsaw is full of these huge billboards: 'Why do we save whales, but kill babies?' 'Abortion: The Bolsheviks' favourite policy.' And 'Abortion for Polish women: legalised by Hitler.'

JAN. Posters saying: 'This is what a cut-up fetus looks like.' That's not a picture of an aborted fetus, that's a dead baby which has been cut up. I know the difference.

MARYSIA. It's a hot day. Thirty degrees. My appointment with Jan's at seven. It's six. I wonder where I can find somewhere with air conditioning. I think about a café, but I don't have any money to waste and anyway I feel sick, like I did before my exams. If I drink anything I'll puke.

JAN. Forceps, kidney dish, disinfectant.

MARYSIA. I go into a church. It's always so nice and cool there. I'm not like Mary's cousin Elizabeth. No angel

appears to me. The baby does not leap in my womb – I speak
straight to the wooden Jesus, straight to his face. His eyes are
closed, as they always are.

JAN. She's fifteen minutes late. It doesn't auger well for a
future assistant, but after that she's never late again.

MARYSIA. Hail Mary, full of grace, the Lord is with thee.
Blessed art thou among women and blessed is the fruit of thy
womb, Jesus. Holy Mary, Mother of God, pray for us sinners
now and at the hour of our death. Amen.

JAN. As she lies there, she tells me a joke. So there's this public
stoning for a sinner. Jesus says – 'Let he who is without sin
throw the first stone.' And suddenly, bang! This stone flies
out of nowhere. And Jesus goes, 'Mum, I told you to stay out
of this!' I like a woman with a sense of humour.

MARYSIA. Afterwards I feel tired, but when I wake up the next
day I'm happy. I should be feeling guilty, like I'm the worst
person in the world, but actually I just feel totally happy and
free. The only syndrome I have is post-joy syndrome. My
life is mine to live again, a stitch in time has saved nine,
nothing has changed. I didn't do it because I'd been raped. I
wasn't. I didn't do it because the baby was sick – it wasn't a
baby, it was part of my body, it was pregnancy tissue. I didn't
do it because my health was at risk. I did it because my
world was at risk.

JAN. Can you start on Monday?

MARYSIA. I took the job, obviously. And I took Jan.
Obviously. I look at him and I can't believe he's real. What
have I done to deserve so much happiness? Why me?

JAN. I took her. I don't know why, but from the very first
moment I saw her I knew: you're going to be mine. It will
bring us together. It will be our secret.

MARYSIA. From that moment on, he starts finding out all sorts
of things about me, because he's not stupid, he's incredibly
intelligent. I'm jealous of every single one of his patients.
They come in, say hello, they go out. Sometimes I count
them. If they reproduced, there would be a whole town's

worth of babies. Whole cities pass through his hands. I want to pretend that the doctor's already gone home for the day. There's been a terrible mistake with your treatment and unfortunately the consequences are totally irreversible. Oh, I'm sorry, the doctor's on holiday at the moment, the doctor actually hanged himself this morning in his garage, leaving behind his ten disabled children, yes, they're all orphans now, that's right, he had a heart attack, a stroke, a roof tile fell on his head. I'm very sorry but the doctor's gone blind so he won't be able to look at your vagina ever again.

JAN *laughs, affectionately, slightly patronisingly.* MARYSIA *looks at him.*

I can't accept the fact that I have to share you with everyone. I want a fat old slob who stays at home in his pyjamas, not someone who's really good-looking and goes abroad to medical conferences. I want him to come home from work at five and never want to go out again in the evenings, I don't want him to care about people, I want the only person who uses him to be me. I'm jealous of his cigarettes – that it's them between his lips and not me. My love turns me slightly schizophrenic and then, ta-da, I get the first letter from Mum since I've been in Warsaw:

JAN *holds a letter in his hands – he reads in the voice of* MARYSIA*'s mother, like someone who has inadvertently found a personal letter.*

JAN. Dear Marysia, how are you? You have been in my prayers!

MARYSIA. I feel so sad. Things are great, Mum.

JAN. I prayed that you would arrive safely. You've already phoned, so I can relax now. My blood pressure's two hundred over three hundred. I was wondering. Do you think you could send us a thousand złoty?

MARYSIA. A thousand złoty? That's what I earn in a month. Before tax.

JAN. Or one thousand five hundred? Then we could pay the rent. We've fallen behind. Won't you help your nearest and dearest?

MARYSIA. And where am I meant to get this money from? Do you think I shit cash?

JAN. I'm sure you'll help us. After all, that's how I raised you.

MARYSIA. I was raised by the TV.

JAN. I walked in to town today to save the price of the bus ticket.

MARYSIA. She's so ridiculous.

JAN. I know, I know, I thought to myself, 'I'm being ridiculous,' but your father is the one who's really ridiculous around here, stuffing matchsticks into the holes in the shower to stop the water running out. I think that's being ridiculous. I say to him, Marek, get a grip on yourself.

MARYSIA. God give me strength.

JAN. And then I thought, if you're getting settled in Warsaw, maybe your sister could come and live with you and go to college or something there?

MARYSIA. And how am I meant to pay for her trousers and shampoo? I'm still a child myself.

JAN. At the end of the day, she's your sister. Won't you help your nearest and dearest? I have to tell you something – I was weak today. I've given up chocolate for Lent but your father brought a box home from work. Well – we're only human at the end of the day.

MARYSIA. No comment.

JAN. I read an interesting article about contraception in my *Catholic Love* magazine, it was in the 'John Paul the Second's Generation' section. It was very good. As you know, I have a negative attitude to contraception.

MARYSIA. Oh, for God's sake…

JAN. I never take precautions. My conscience wouldn't let me. Your father laughs at me. 'Natural family planning is all right if you're in *Dynasty*, but not for people who have jobs to go to.' And he rolls his condom on.

MARYSIA. I don't want to hear this!

JAN. The end of the world is nigh. It's all happening exactly as the Holy Father said it would. Earthquakes, tsunamis, abortions – the value of life is being eclipsed by the culture of death.

God bless you,

Mum.

MARYSIA. It goes on like that for seven years. I call her sometimes.

One December I lie and say I've been asked to work so much overtime that I won't be able to come home for Christmas. I send her fifty złoty and I get some peace and quiet. If anyone found these letters, I would die of shame.

JAN. Interesting, very interesting.

MARYSIA. You read my letters? You bastard!

JAN. I know everything about you. Why don't you just tell her what you actually think for once?

MARYSIA. If I told my mother what I actually thought, I'd need to take a pack of Valium, a pack of ibuprofen, a can of Red Bull and a litre of vodka. The only reason I don't take heroin is cos it's too expensive. Or I'd need a therapist! Which I can't afford either.

JAN. Verily, verily I say unto you: I am your therapist. I am your guardian angel. I will cure you. I will give you to eat, I will give you to drink, I will change your nappy and I will rock you in my arms. I will make sure you are not frightened, I will hold your hand so you cannot fall, from me you will receive bread and milk, with me you will watch the best films and I will show you the most beautiful places on Earth. I am warm, I can cope with the world, with me you will find your 'definitely', with me you will have your 'for ever'. You can hit me and I will never strike back. You can spit on me and I will never spit back. If you curse me, I will call you 'darling'. If you die, I will lay myself next to you in your grave.

MARYSIA. Sometimes when he's doing the washing up, his face is reflected in a knife. I position myself so I can see it. If I took it in my hand. If. I love that mouth and that nose so much I almost hate them. I could cut them off and carry them round in my wallet.

Why I want to kill you:

Because you're so kind, you check four times to see if I've got milk in my coffee.

Because you tell me to go and get you cigarettes and keep the change.

Because I have two worn-out bras and I'm embarrassed to undress in front of you.

Because you're like a clenched fist and I can't prise you open.

Because you have an entire past without me, and I don't have any past at all without you.

Because you doubt me, and I never doubt you.

Because you don't want me to have you.

Because you're a criminal.

Because you spit on my God, but He exists.

And because you're your son's father.

Scene Five

15th August 2010. Niepokalanów. Outside the church.

JAN. You can't look at his cards if you're on the same team as him!

MARYSIA. What are you talking about? How can I be on his team if there's only three of us? Why are you even putting us in teams?

JAN. All right, forget it. This is meant to be fun, I want him to see what a great present he's got. You start.

MARYSIA (*holding a card in her hand*). Okay. This is where you've come from.

PIOTR. Mum's farm?

JAN. Really?

MARYSIA. Before that.

PIOTR. The airport.

MARYSIA. Yes but where from?

PIOTR. London.

MARYSIA. More generally?

PIOTR. The middle of nowhere. I'm joking. Western Europe. The West. Bingo! My turn. (*Takes a card.*) Okay. When we were walking round Trafalgar Square, this is the illness you said you were most scared of.

MARYSIA. AIDS.

PIOTR (*pulling out the next card*). Anal?

MARYSIA. Beads.

JAN. All right, that's enough. I hope you like it. It's just a token, you'll get your real one later. How are you, son? Another year older, eh?

PIOTR. I'm brilliant. Fantastic. Perfect. You?

JAN. I have cancer, but I came anyway.

PIOTR. Oh my God. What kind?

JAN. Oesophageal. With some metastases to my liver. And my bones. They're black on the inside. They've removed one of my lungs.

PIOTR. Jesus.

JAN. Didn't you tell him?

MARYSIA. No. I forgot.

Beat.

JAN. Just kidding. Don't they have jokes in London?

PIOTR (*giving him a packet*). Here. This is from your wife.

JAN. Your mum? Please pass on my thanks. (*Gives the package to MARYSIA.*)

PIOTR. Aren't you going to go and see her? It's only fifteen minutes down the road.

JAN. No.

PIOTR. The organic farm's doing really well. It's done her a lot of good to come back here, don't you think?

JAN. Of course. It's never too late to do something with your life, even if you're in your late forties.

'I don't see why you should bother working,' I said to her, a long time ago. 'You've never really liked being an architect, why not just enjoy your life? Be a lady of leisure.' I was being sarcastic, but unfortunately for me she took me at my word. I don't think there's any point in me working either, she said. And she stuck to that for the next twenty years. What's she given me?

MARYSIA (*looking in the bag*). Deep-fried cock.

PIOTR. I had to go and see her because she'd asked me to bring her some shoes from Primark. Seven pairs.

MARYSIA (*to* JAN). Primark's that shop where you find the severed fingers of Chinese children mixed up with the cheap pants.

JAN. Is she living by herself?

MARYSIA. What do you care?

PIOTR. No. She's got four cats, two dogs, a tortoise and a boa constrictor that she bought a week ago. He seems very nice.

JAN. Where does she keep it?

MARYSIA. Is that important?

PIOTR. In her yoga room.

JAN. How lovely. But listen now – what day is it today?

MARYSIA. The Feast of the Assumption of our Blessed Lady Mary.

JAN. Wrong. We're celebrating a different occasion.

PIOTR. In the Congo, they're celebrating Independence Day. In Korea, it's Liberation Day. It's the anniversary of Macbeth's death and on this day we also celebrate the birthdays of Napoleon Bonaparte, Ben Affleck and... me!

JAN pulls out a cake box and hands it to MARYSIA.

JAN. Happy birthday to our very own St Pete! You can blow your candles out in a minute. (*To* MARYSIA.) Will you cut it up?

MARYSIA. 'Happy Christening, Jakub'? What have you bought?

JAN. It was on special offer. Someone had ordered it and never come to collect it. I just thought it was so lovely that I had to buy it. Anyway, what does it matter what it says? We all know what the occasion is.

PIOTR looks at the baby made of icing.

PIOTR. Is that a baby made of icing? It must have taken ages!

JAN (*to* MARYSIA). Cut it up. Go on. (*To* PIOTR.) And you blow up the balloons.

MARYSIA. I'd rather we did it the other way round. (*Blows up a balloon.*) I don't have anything for you. Just many happy returns.

PIOTR. Well, I've got something for you! Sobranie Cocktail Cigarettes. All the colours of the rainbow. You wanted to buy a packet, remember? I just wish they didn't have these photos of lung cancer all over them. It's so disgusting. And so was the plane. Full of Poles. Embarrassing Poles. You would not believe how badly we're represented abroad, seriously. Fat pigs and red-faced plumbers. I chose business-class on purpose so I wouldn't have to come into contact with them – and what do you know, there weren't any tickets left. And then I ended up sitting next to a baby who screamed the whole way over. I could have killed it. Smothered it with my coat.

MARYSIA. The bridges in London are amazing… One day I'm going to design bridges exactly like that.

JAN. Ah yes, but who built those bridges for them? Poles. You and me. (*Pointing at* MARYSIA.) Your dad and your brother, who fly over on their cheap Wizz Air flights. Your grandfather and your great-grandfather. I don't want to sound rude but who do they think built Buckingham Palace for them?

PIOTR. Well, Dad? How does it feel to get back to your roots?

JAN. These festivals are for those perverts in their black dresses. Well, I'll tell you something. Their precious Polish Pope wasn't so saintly.

MARYSIA. Stop it!

JAN. He smuggled his mistress into the Vatican so she could read the Bible to him at night. The Catholic Church are to blame for everything. They're fanatics. 'Poland is a Catholic country!' It's all I hear. 'I'm Catholic, you're Catholic, she's Catholic, he's Catholic.' 'We have to compromise with the Church.' The Church, the Church, everywhere I go there's the Church. It's talking on TV, it's talking at gynaecology conferences, feminists are talking with the Church – this is meant to be a secular country and we sign a concordat with the Vatican. It makes me sick. Read Freud, and then you'll realise that they're all paedophiles who were spoilt by their mothers!

PIOTR (*to* MARYSIA, *referring to the cigarettes*). Aren't you having one? They're good for the nerves.

MARYSIA. No.

JAN. No, she's been very clean-living for a month now. She doesn't smoke, doesn't drink. She came to you in trainers, and she left in Louboutins. London obviously went to her head!

PIOTR. I went all over Soho and Camden looking for these! Come on, have one. Just a quick drag.

MARYSIA. Why are you doing this to me?

JAN. He can't do anything to you. Just ignore him! Be smarter than him.

PIOTR. Come on, let's get a beer. My round. Ah, fresh Polish air, we should bottle this stuff and sell it to Londoners in their organic shops. A clear blue sky – we could flog that to them and all. Aren't you excited, Dad?

MARYSIA (*to herself, playing with the balloon*). And I'm pregnant.

JAN. I'd be happier if some people were a little less excited.

MARYSIA (*to herself*). And I'm pregnant.

JAN. And I don't really drink alcohol.

MARYSIA. Yeah right.

JAN. But I'll drink to your health today. I'm the father of the family.

MARYSIA (*to herself; she pops the balloon she was playing with*). And I'm pregnant!

PIOTR. What do you say? Do you fancy a little something?

MARYSIA. Yes. A very little something.

Scene Six

May 2010. Warsaw. JAN*'s surgery.*

MARYSIA. Three months earlier. Back in Warsaw.

PIOTR. Three months earlier.

> Dad talks me into going home for a week. I say yes. I go. And there she is.

MARYSIA. I'm sitting in my boss's surgery, taking care of his kingdom, like the little office tart, like a deflated balloon. My boyfriend's cross because none of the women I'm registering want to sign up for his full nine-month pregnancy and birth service. They only want to make the one appointment.

> (*As though she were on the phone:*) Are you calling about the advert? 'Pharmaceutical gynaecology – solutions to help you get your life back on track!' 'Women's health services: helping you deal with unexpected situations your own way.'

PIOTR. Well well well, what do we have here then? She's changed.

MARYSIA. That's right. We have the full range of gynaecological drugs. It's a safe and effective way of restoring your menstrual cycle. The service costs two thousand złoty, and we don't send an invoice or bill. We can cleanse you from Monday to Friday, think of it as being dirty, darling, think of it as a piece of dirt inside you. We don't carry out any procedures on Saturdays or Sundays because we like to keep the holy day holy.

PIOTR. Let's go and get a coffee.

MARYSIA. I don't like coffee.

PIOTR. So let's go and get a raspberry smoothie.

MARYSIA. I don't like smoothies either.

PIOTR. So let's go and get a hot chocolate. And a doughnut.
And a croissant. A guy comes home once a year and no one
can even bring themselves to have a coffee with him. Dad's
had enough for today. He's given me some cash. Come on,
let's go and spend it. He wants to be alone. You haven't
changed a bit! Are you still seventeen? (*Sings.*) 'Young and
sweet, only seventeen, oh yeeeeaaahhhh!'

MARYSIA. I'm actually twenty-five and unlike you I'm not a
child any more, I'm a grown woman.

PIOTR. I'm certainly not a woman, I'm not going to contradict
you there.

The phone rings. PIOTR *answers it and doesn't let*
MARYSIA *get to it.*

Hello? Yes, this is his surgery. Of course you can make an
appointment. What's the problem? Your pills have run out?
Oh dear, that's no good, is it? We all need to be able to
express our love, don't we? Absolutely. Please abstain for the
time being. In half an hour? Of course, we'll have them
ready for you. When your husband comes back, you'll be
able to do it nice and slow and long. How do I like doing it?
That all depends on who I'm with. Your favourite assistant
can't come to the phone right now because she's being
interviewed by the *Guardian*. They think she's a really
interesting person. People are going crazy for her right now,
you know. What's that? She's beautiful and magnetic? Oh, I
quite agree. If you can manage to come by later today, you
should still catch her, but I'm not sure if she'll be around
after that because I've just asked her to go on holiday with
me to London. (*Hangs up.*)

You're an angel. That's what Dad always says and I can see
what he means. So what do you say? Will you come to
London?

MARYSIA. What's it like? What's there to see?

PIOTR. War, pestilence and famine.

MARYSIA. I envy you. I wish London was so familiar to me I
was getting sick of it.

PIOTR. I envy you. I wish London was still the object of my fantasies.

MARYSIA. Why are you touching me? It's a sin.

PIOTR. It's not me. It's my hand.

MARYSIA (*to* JAN). I'd like to ask you for two weeks' holiday.

JAN. What for?

MARYSIA. I'd like to go on holiday. Your son's invited me to London.

JAN. Well, you should go. See a bit of the world. Travel broadens the mind. Tell you what, I'll even give you a bonus. And I can give you something towards the cost of the ticket. It'll be good for him to see a familiar face. He's a smart one all right. Takes after his dad! I was drunk when he was conceived, you know.

MARYSIA. What had you drunk?

JAN. It must have been something good, because he's doing brilliantly now. (*Hands her a bank note, says goodbye to her and waves.*)

MARYSIA. I start missing him as soon as I leave the room. But I keep going.

Scene Seven

May 2010. London.

MARYSIA *is wearing the kind of accessories people wear when they're trying to look cool – sunglasses, neck scarf, etc.*

MARYSIA. I go and I can't believe my eyes. Sophia Loren sings 'Felicità' in my head. The first thing I think is: 'Oh, Poland, you damp, faintly soggy country, why don't you have bridges like this? Why don't you have TV shows like this?' The mornings here are so beautiful, and the exhaust fumes smell like candyfloss! The traffic jams are amazing! The puddles are gigantic! And the second thing I notice is him. He's different. He looks a bit like Jesus.

PIOTR. How's your hotel? I booked the best one in town.

MARYSIA. It's amazing. I drank all the miniatures from the minibar, and when I came back, they'd reproduced! It's a miracle! Is everything here like that?

PIOTR. Everything. Come on, let's go into town and you can see for yourself. These are my friends, we just all kind of hang out together, yeah, whatever, it's cool. Guys, this is my girlfriend.

MARYSIA. Okay, I'm not going to contradict him…

PIOTR. My old life was just so boring, do you know what I mean? But things are sweet here, yeah? I don't speak Polish any more, babes. Piotr is gone. I'm Peter now. I'm bisexual, you know. I've finally realised.

MARYSIA. That's a sin. But fine, whatever, I'm not going to say anything. There's so much to do here! How do you manage to study?

PIOTR. Who needs to study? Personality is the only thing that really matters.

MARYSIA. It's so beautiful here! Everything's all perfumed and shiny, I wish I'd been born here!

PIOTR. Fancy something to eat?

MARYSIA. Can we have fish and chips?

PIOTR (*as though to a waiter*). My companion will have the fish and chips, please! Hold on, what's this? Excuse me, this is cold, and it's a tiny portion. Do you know who this lady is? She's a distant relative of Kate Middleton, you know! Could we get some caviar as well, please, and some sushi and two London Cosmopolitans to quench our thirst. Cheers! Hey, the guys are asking you what you want to be when you grow up.

MARYSIA. I don't know. Workers' children become workers, doctors' children become doctors. So I'm probably going to be a postman or the woman who does the flowers in church. I missed the deadline for architecture again this year. I'm going to apply again next year though.

PIOTR. If you think I'm going to become a doctor like my gran and my granddad and my dad, you're wrong. I'm going to be king of the world! And you don't need any shitty qualifications for that. You could be a violinist, you have such delicate hands…

MARYSIA. If you want to be a violinist, you have to start by the time you're six. It's a bit late for me now.

PIOTR. The guys want to know what your life motto is. Say it in Polish, I'll translate for them.

MARYSIA. Life's just one big shit and you don't get another one. Life, not shit.

PIOTR *laughs,* MARYSIA *is pleased too.*

Thanks for inviting me to come and stay with you.

PIOTR. Never thank anyone for anything. I was thinking… why don't you stay a bit longer? We've only got a week left. That's not enough time. We still have to go for a beer with Prince Harry! I'll call Dad and say you want to stay for another two weeks.

MARYSIA. I don't know. I miss him.

PIOTR. Ah, come on, just stay.

JAN. I try and avoid all that computer rubbish as much as possible. It rots the brain. And the radiation can be harmful. But the week she's away, I join Facebook. I create a false account which I call 'The Julia Roberts Fan Club'. I send them both friend requests and they accept. Then I look at all their stupid photos: waving, laughing, eating ice cream, kissing each other on the cheek. It gets to me, I have to say. So I send her a text message: 'Darling, I'm not coping. Please come home. I need you.'

PIOTR. Here you go, another London Cosmopolitan. Is it good? Tell him: there's still so much we have to see. I'll be back in three weeks.

MARYSIA. I don't know…

PIOTR. Just delete it. Look. It's easy: you just press here.

MARYSIA. No…

PIOTR. It's easy.

> MARYSIA *deletes the text message.*

> See? That wasn't hard, was it? Laters, Daddy! Do you want anything else?

MARYSIA. Chocolate.

PIOTR. In moments of despair, poor people eat chocolate.

> PIOTR *is slightly drunk. He lies down.* MARYSIA *approaches him and inspects his body. She drinks her London Cosmopolitan.*

MARYSIA. I like alcohol. When I drink, my brain's full of blue and my eyes are full of green. At home, I never drank, so now I'm making up for lost time. Cheers! I look at his face after our night of London Cosmopolitans. He has his father's nose. His father's chin. His eyebrows, his mouth, his mole. Everything.

PIOTR. Dad said you were a lot like his last assistant.

MARYSIA. I didn't know he'd had another assistant.

PIOTR. He's had at least four. He's been around for a long time, you know. He's not the freshest blood the family has to offer. But I meant that as a compliment – his last one looked like a seventeen-year-old Madonna. Or like a young version of Mum.

MARYSIA. Was she a bitch as well?

PIOTR. She was pretty. Last time Dad met up with Mum, to talk about where I might do my PhD, he called me up afterwards and said: 'She might not have a brain, but I have to say she's looking good for her age.'

MARYSIA. I wish I could say the same for him. He's an old man. I've spent seven years of my life with a manky old man! His hands are covered in liver spots, and they're dry from the constant washing. He's got a humpback and varicose veins and false teeth and he's going bald and his breath stinks in the morning. He looks like a tree. An old tree, an oak. (*Touches* PIOTR.)

PIOTR. Why are you touching me?

MARYSIA. It's not me, it's my hand. (*To herself.*) God, make me stop wanting this man. And as for the other one – make me stop missing him. (*To* PIOTR.) Touch me.

PIOTR. It's a sin.

MARYSIA. It's only a sin if you're married…

PIOTR. Well, if you put it like that…

MARYSIA. Jack and Jill go up the hill. Easy peasy lemon squeezy. Dogs mate, rabbits breed, and human beings whore themselves. And where better to whore yourself than London?

A beam of light falls from on high.

Oh God! I know this isn't very holy. But you should have thought about that before you infected me with original sin, shouldn't you? So – tough.

PIOTR *sits and watches* MARYSIA, *who slowly takes her clothes off. It's somewhere between a dance and an awkward striptease, but* PIOTR *likes it.*

And above us, around us and in us – is God.

PIOTR. Take that off.

MARYSIA. God lies between his thighs. He even stands to attention.

PIOTR. Kick that over there.

MARYSIA. God lives between my breasts.

PIOTR. Spread your legs.

MARYSIA. And everything is holy if it reflects human nature and our desire to eat and kiss.

PIOTR. Put your hands on the wall.

MARYSIA. The third deadly sin: lust.

PIOTR. Bend over.

MARYSIA. The fourth: gluttony.

Only now does PIOTR *touch her. It's brutal, more brutal than anything she's experienced before.*

PIOTR. Wow. Amazing. Really, really. You've got such pretty eyes…

MARYSIA. Oh, come on. 'Pretty eyes'? The truth is: Me woman, you man. It's a bit of hormones, that's all. What's the date today?

PIOTR. Does that matter? I've had a lovely day. And you're got lovely eyes.

MARYSIA. The fourteenth. Fuck!

PIOTR. Is it Valentine's Day?

MARYSIA. It's May, you idiot. (*To herself.*) History likes to repeat itself, doesn't it. You stupid, stupid idiot – where did you leave your brain? Did they confiscate it at the airport? I know what's going to happen, I can already feel something growing inside me, just like I did then. I'm super-fertile, I've hunted out a male to mate with as though I were an animal. I wish I could stop myself wanting to touch people, I wish no one smelled good to me. What about architecture, what about

my unbuilt bridges? I know I'm going to conceive. Twenty-
five years old. Education: none. Family: none. Talent: none.
Plans: none. Mother Nature just gets on with it all by herself.
She does the thinking for me. She says: 'See, now you're
going to be important, now you'll have something to live for.'
Maybe it's for the best. It's been fun but there have to be
consequences. My life was totally, completely meaningless.
No one would have cried for me. So I'm going to make sure
I have someone who'll cry for me. And then my life will
have a meaning. It's time you got some self-respect, you
little slut. It's time to become a mother!

Scene Eight

May 2010, the last day of MARYSIA's *holiday. London, the*
airport.

MARYSIA. Are you all right? You're as white as a sheet.

PIOTR. It's because you're leaving. Airports are the saddest
places in the world.

MARYSIA. What do the English say when they bump into each
other on the street? If there's a collision?

PIOTR. They'd probably say: 'Oh, I'm sorry, how are you?' and
then: 'I'm fine, you've crushed my foot, have a nice day.'

MARYSIA. They don't get angry?

PIOTR. No.

MARYSIA. And what do you say if you've got a surprise for
someone?

PIOTR. I don't know. There's probably some pun or play on
words they use.

MARYSIA. I want to have a cat with you.

PIOTR. A cat? I don't even trust myself to buy a pot plant from
Ikea. You've got to water them, plant them out…

MARYSIA. Cats are great. You can hold them. You should have physical contact with another person or an animal three times a day or else you'll get cancer.

PIOTR. I'm going to get cancer anyway. Today I'll go out, get drunk and forget about everything, and then I'll wake up tomorrow, remember it all and have to go out and get drunk again.

MARYSIA. Don't you want to have a cat?

PIOTR. No.

Are you glad you're leaving? Your gate's closing. You'll have to do the next bit alone. Here – (*Gives her twenty pounds.*) get yourself something nice in duty free, a souvenir or something.

MARYSIA. Have you got a cigarette?

PIOTR. The thing with cigarettes is that they're gone before you know it.

MARYSIA. Just like love.

PIOTR. And they cause cancer and heart disease.

MARYSIA. Just like love.

PIOTR. I might buy you a cat. I'll think about it.

MARYSIA. Is there anything you want to ask me?

PIOTR. What does it say over there? 'Shalom'? What does that mean?

MARYSIA. Fuck off.

PIOTR. Fuck off? In Hebrew?

MARYSIA. Yes. Fuck off.

PIOTR (*to the audience*). It's so stupid – you meet someone and they're great, maybe they have a really nice way of saying their 'r's or something, and all you want to do is listen and listen to it, and then before you know it there's a total stranger standing in front of you wanting things from you. What I want to know is: why would anyone want anything from me? Who do they think I am, Bob Geldof? Is it really that strange? Has no one in the history of the world ever come home, looked at the person standing there in their slippers saying: 'Hello, love, how was your day?' and thought, why am I with this person and not one of the other seven billion people out there? How am I meant to know who I should be with? How am I meant to know which flat I should rent? This one might be the best one. Or there might be a better one seven streets away. As soon as you fall in love with someone, what happens? You get bored of them and you fall in love with someone else. How can I know anything for sure? Did Michael Jackson OD or was he killed? I don't know. Do I love her, do I love her not – I don't know. But I know what I do want: I want my suitcase to be packed and waiting. Twenty-four hours a day. I want to come home from my two weeks in Paris Madrid Moscow and find a loaf of mouldy bread in the bread bin and a carton of sour milk in the fridge. I want to forget to pack my toothbrush and my toothpaste and my slippers. That's what I want. I don't want to be like my father, in his surgery from eight in the morning to eight at night, five days a week.

Scene Nine

Two hours later. Warsaw.

MARYSIA. I fly back to Warsaw. In my head there's a funeral march playing.

JAN. Her plane's delayed by fifteen minutes. I can already see it all: it's crashed, she's dead, now what am I going to do? Turns out it was just fog.

MARYSIA. During a two-hour flight, I age fifteen years. By the time I land, I've gone grey inside.

JAN. Something's wrong. (*To* MARYSIA.) Hi.

MARYSIA. Jan looks better than ever. Not handsome so much as beautiful, like a Saint in a painting. He scratches his chin and it's the best sound in the world. (*To* JAN.) Hi.

JAN. She's been warmed by a different sun. Whipped by a different wind.

MARYSIA. He doesn't say anything. I don't say anything. I don't touch him, because if I did it would hurt so much my heart would break.

JAN. Nothing, not even a flicker of greeting.

MARYSIA. He looks like a child who needs a hug. I don't look at him, because if I did my eyes would explode.

JAN. She turns her head away, as though she had something to hide.

MARYSIA. I smell my clothes.

JAN. She smells of the great wide world.

MARYSIA. I smell my hands. They smell of sin. And then I'm back in the toilet, back with the fear, the biggest fear in the world, waiting for lines to appear on a plastic stick: is it going to be one line or two, one, two, one, two? Two. TWO.

So it's true. I knew anyway. But I'm still in shock. My heart's pounding. I send a text and I know it'll be a slap in the face for him: 'I'm late.'

PIOTR. Shit.

Scene Ten

15th August 2010. Niepokalanów. Outside the church.

JAN (*with a Taboo card in his hand*). She doesn't have any wrinkles. She does yoga, t'ai chi, goes to mass and is doing a course in Satanism for beginners.

PIOTR. You only bought me this game because you wanted to play it yourself, didn't you? I think it's boring.

JAN. What did you talk about with Mummy?

PIOTR. I told her that you always support me and she never does.

JAN. But she's the one you run to first… You know what your problem is? You're spoilt.

PIOTR *pulls out a small bottle of vodka and pours them each a glass.*

PIOTR. I need to talk to you. I brought something along for the grown-ups.

JAN. Doesn't Marysia count?

PIOTR. She's the baby of the group.

JAN. Actually, she's not.

PIOTR. All right, Dad, don't be such a pedant.

JAN. All right, son, I won't. Why don't you tell me what you'd like for your birthday instead? Apart from the game, I mean.

PIOTR. There's not really anything I want.

JAN. You're my pride and joy. The apple of my eye. Everyone else just wants to milk me dry. You're the only one who's making his own way. So tell me what you want.

PIOTR. All right then. Can I get a Porsche?

JAN. A Porsche is the kind of present you get when you're my age.

PIOTR. Then I'd like a million dollars.

JAN. I'd write you a cheque, but I've forgotten my diamond fountain pen.

PIOTR. In that case, let's make the sum slightly lower. How about five thousand pounds?

JAN. Have the cheese sandwiches on campus got more expensive?

PIOTR. Two and a half?

JAN. I pay your rent. I pay your bills. What else do you need? You're studying at one of the best colleges in the UK. You're going to be a lawyer. I envy you.

PIOTR. What's so good about being a lawyer?

JAN. You can heal our wild, sick country.

PIOTR. People are always going to kill each other in their own homes. Doctors will always commit crimes. People will always steal chocolate bars from Tesco. I'm not going to change anything.

JAN. You could change the law. You could be the one.

PIOTR. Do you believe in the law?

JAN. I don't believe in what we call laws in this country. But I believe in the idea of the law.

PIOTR. All right, then tell me something. In the UK, it's legal to cross the road when the light's red. And do they have more corpses on their roads than we do? No, they have fewer. In Berlin, it's legal to drink alcohol on the street, and does that mean they have a higher rate of alcoholism than in Warsaw?

No, it means theirs is lower. I've been thinking a lot about things like that.

JAN. It's good to question things.

PIOTR. Maybe you should try it sometimes. Mum's not actually doing very well, by the way.

JAN. Is that my fault?

PIOTR. No. Nothing's ever your fault, is it? Like the fact that I couldn't write an essay for college for a whole year. Nothing to do with you.

JAN. Why didn't you tell me?

PIOTR. Why didn't you ask? We had to write an essay on ethics. The only thing I could think about was medical ethics. But what could I say about that?

JAN. They give you some stupid essay questions in that country. But how did you do? Did you get an A?

PIOTR. No.

JAN. A B? A B's fine too. You can't always be top. I think I could even deal with a C-plus, although I know you'd be disappointed with that.

PIOTR. They chucked me out.

Beat.

JAN. They did what? I've been having problems with my middle ear recently. Can you say that again?

PIOTR. They threw me out.

JAN. When?

PIOTR. Two years ago. I wasn't good enough. Or talented enough. Or clever enough.

JAN. I've been paying your rent for the last three years. Six hundred pounds a month. Six hundred times twelve times three plus tuition fees plus bills, food and new shoes – how much does that come to? You can still add up, can't you? Where's my money?

PIOTR. I squandered it. I was young and stupid.

JAN. You did pass your school exams, didn't you?

PIOTR. I got my international baccalaureate. You know that.

JAN. I thought I did but now I'm not so sure. Maybe I just paid
for you to get a piece of paper. What about primary school –
did you finish that? Or was that all a lie too? Do you even
know how to write? Maybe it was me who paid for all those
certificates you have, eh? Or did you just take my money and
pretend then too?

Beat.

Why is everyone so disappointing?

PIOTR. I ask myself the same thing sometimes. But your
child's your child, right?

JAN. Children just happen to a man sometimes. Do you have
any savings?

PIOTR. Savings?

JAN. An account? Stocks and shares?

PIOTR. I'm twenty-five years old.

JAN. Exactly. When I was your age I had my medical licence
and a child on the way. From today, I'm turning off the tap.
I'd start worrying if I were you.

PIOTR. I've got other things to worry about. There's this girl.
We don't see each other very often, but when we do, we
make the most of it. And…well… we made too much of it.

JAN. Well, I'm sorry but that definitely isn't my fault. Do I
know her?

PIOTR. Yes.

JAN. Well?

PIOTR. What do you think? (*Beat.*) Yes, you know her well.
Very well. Will you help us?

JAN. No.

PIOTR. Talk to her. Persuade her. You can do it. I can't.

JAN. No.

PIOTR. Why not?

JAN. Because it would be a waste of good genes.

PIOTR. You're crazy. Who are you? What do you think? What do you feel? What films do you like, what music are you in to, what's your favourite colour? I don't know anything about you.

JAN. I like the films of Federico Fellini. My favourite music would be Franz Schubert. And my favourite colour is grey.

PIOTR. Am I your punishment for something? Am I your failure? Would you have preferred to have a daughter? Is that what all this is about, this girl who's come between us, is this whole thing about you wanting a daughter?

JAN. No.

PIOTR. Because… you know what? You know what I think? I think there's a divine particle in each one of us: in her, in me, everywhere. Do you understand? There's a divine particle. God is blood, God is the strength that means we can move and breathe.

JAN. That's a dogma. I don't do dogmas. God, what God. I always write it with a small 'g' and say it with a small 'g'.

PIOTR. And ultimately, you're destroying that power. You've been destroying it and turning it to mush for years. At school when they asked me what my dad did I said: he's a dentist. A surgeon. A cardiologist. A dermatologist. Does he treat athlete's foot? Yes, that's what he does. He treats athlete's foot and rashes and boils. Anything. Anything other than that –

JAN. Than what?

PIOTR. Than that. Mum always said: 'Daddy does bad things. Don't go in there and show him your report card with all the 'A's. He's cutting off heads right now, he's torturing and killing.'

JAN. Then why do you want to do the same thing now?

PIOTR. Because I'm a stupid, immature little boy. I don't know what I'm doing. I'm panicking. I want to have the world all to myself. I don't want a little version of my body walking about. I don't want it to grow. I don't want it to live in this place. I don't want it to remember you. I don't want it to be half her.

JAN. Why not? She's pretty. She's good. She's the best. If I were twenty years younger…

PIOTR. But you aborted her child.

JAN. I did it once. I don't want to do it again.

PIOTR. Talk to her. Persuade her. It'll be the last thing I'll ever ask you to do for me. I'll never ask you for anything else ever again.

JAN. No.

PIOTR. If I was twenty years older and I'd been to Miami, Florida, China, Iceland, if I'd eaten all the food in the world, if I'd smelled all the kinds of air, seen every sunset on every continent… If. But not now. Is that the right decision? Tell me.

JAN. I don't know. You're an adult now, I'm afraid. Sorry.

PIOTR (*to himself*). Why I want to kill you:

Because it wasn't you who got me a Tamagotchi for my birthday, it was Mum.

Because I make the same spelling mistakes you do.

Because you've got more hair than I do and I wish your hairline would recede more.

Because you're always better.

Because I never know how much you know.

Because I don't know who I'm going to be in the future.

Because there's not a single place on Earth that I really like and that's your fault.

Because you remind me of Poland.

And because you brought her into our lives.

Scene Eleven

15th August 2010. Niepokalanów. Church.

PIOTR. You're not going to come out, are you? You're going to hide in here all day.

MARYSIA. You can talk to me, but you can't do anything to me. It's forbidden in churches. This is where the cursed and the exiled and the banished come for sanctuary.

PIOTR. I don't want to do anything to you.

MARYSIA. People like you shouldn't be allowed in here.

PIOTR. Neither should people like you. What do you think you're doing? 'I'm pregnant and I'm staying that way'? What kind of a text is that?

MARYSIA. Why are you talking about this with me in here?

PIOTR. It's not just your decision. It's my decision too. Fifty per cent.

MARYSIA. Well, why don't you take fifty per cent of the baby and walk around with it inside you and then we can talk. Why shouldn't I do this?

PIOTR. You can do what you want with your fifty per cent but you've got to destroy my genes. Do you think it's moral to walk around with something inside you that you stole from me?

MARYSIA. A new life has started and you don't have the right to destroy it. I wonder if it'll be a boy or a girl. If it'll look like me or you.

PIOTR. I hear you weren't always so pro-life.

MARYSIA. How do you know about that?

PIOTR. I dreamed that you were standing with Jesus and he was whispering something into your ear. You were seventeen.

And you were standing in a pool of raspberry juice. You were just standing there, seventeen years old, looking at this pool of raspberry juice.

MARYSIA (*about* JAN). That bastard. He told you.

PIOTR. He told me, and I told him.

Beat.

MARYSIA. Was he pleased?

PIOTR. I think he was. Because he said he wouldn't intervene.

MARYSIA. So I can count on him sometimes after all. The 'neon nail varnish and crazy-coloured tights' stage of my life is over. I don't want that any more. My brain's going to waste. My body's going to waste. I want to go home, and I mean a proper home, my own home, not a rented room in a flat. I don't want to be forty years old and living by myself in a rented flat with a tortoise and a boa constrictor. This is God's will.

PIOTR. God's?

MARYSIA. He's given me this one in exchange for the other one.

PIOTR. Well then, why don't you call the Holy Spirit and ask him if he's the father? Because you know what, 'father's not a word that really suits me. I've never even thought about it and I've got no intention of thinking about it for a long time yet.

MARYSIA. You don't have to think about it, but I do. You'll be fertile until you're eighty, but I've only got until I'm forty, and one day my eggs are going to turn around and say: 'Nah, sorry, can't be bothered any more.' You're not going to persuade me. I'm one hundred per cent fertile, from top to bottom, and this is the right time. There's a time for binge-drinking and a time for abstinence, a time to kill and a time to give birth, a time to be pert and a time to let yourself go. Why shouldn't I do this?

PIOTR. Because I like getting served in cafés. And wearing nice shoes. I like being able to leave huge tips in restaurants, I like being Julia Roberts. Don't you want to be Julia Roberts?

MARYSIA. Yes.

PIOTR. You see? Everyone wants to be Julia Roberts.

MARYSIA. But I'm not Julia Roberts and I never will be. Why shouldn't I do this?

PIOTR. Because I don't want to do it. I'm genetically predisposed to win Nobel Prizes, not to reproduce.

MARYSIA. That's crap.

PIOTR. I don't know if it's mine or his.

MARYSIA. It's yours.

PIOTR. Are you sure?

MARYSIA. Although it would be a lot better if it was his.

PIOTR. Do you like doing it with married men?

MARYSIA. Do you like doing it with your father's girlfriends? At least you know with married men that they're not gay.

PIOTR. That's their loss. How would you like to be cheated on?

MARYSIA. I'm young. I'm the person people cheat on their partners with. The time will come when I'll be the one being cheated on.

PIOTR. I've got a boyfriend.

MARYSIA. You'll turn normal again one day. I'd wait for you, but the more I listen to you, the less I want to.

PIOTR. Do you like sucking him off?

MARYSIA. I love it.

PIOTR. Especially when he pays you for it.

MARYSIA. Do you like bumming your boyfriends?

PIOTR. You need to be a bit more tolerant, you little homophobe.

MARYSIA. So do you. You come here with your fancy new iPhone and you think you're better than your dad and his ancient old Nokia. Well, you're not. I love his old Nokia.

PIOTR. I suppose it pays your bills.

MARYSIA. Would you like it more if I went and worked in
  McDonald's? What would you know about work anyway?
  You haven't done a day's work in your life.

PIOTR. I'm exploring the world.

MARYSIA. Tell me how you want your life to be. In ten years'
  time.

PIOTR. I want to be a film director. I want to make an erotic
  thriller, real proper art-house cinema, very postmodern, bits
  in slow motion, bits in sepia... I want to be healthy. Have
  enough for a pint at King's Cross. A good film now and then.
  Nothing fancy.

MARYSIA. Who will you live with?

PIOTR. By myself.

MARYSIA. Who'll visit you? When you're ill? When you don't
  have the strength to get yourself a bowl to put next to your
  bed when you've got a stomach bug? When you catch AIDS
  off your boyfriends? (*Beat.*) Yesterday I got to hold my
  friend's baby. She's six weeks old. After I'd left them, I spent
  the whole bus journey smelling my hands and my blouse.
  Babies smell so good... Do you know what I mean?

PIOTR. No. Is there anything else you want to ask me?

MARYSIA. You know what you are?

PIOTR. Enlighten me.

MARYSIA. Scum. Tesco economy scum.

Scene Twelve

15th August 2010. Niepokalanów. Outside the church.

JAN. Her face. Her eyes. Her smile. If I could, I would paint her as an icon. My own private, holy icon.

Why I want to kill you:

Because of the way you walk.

Because you do this with your hair.

Because of the roll of fat on your stomach.

Because you'll still be able to see the world when I'm gone.

Because you're so dear to me, and so ungrateful.

Because you fall into my traps so beautifully.

Because you tell lies without even realising.

Because you can't say no to a single thing I ask you.

Because you pray to your God instead of to me.

And because you laugh at the same time as my son.

MARYSIA *enters.*

What's that face for? Do I amuse you? I'm having a great time here. There are some very interesting people walking about. I'm enjoying just sitting about wasting time.

JAN *drinks.*

MARYSIA. You're going to have a heart attack one day if you're not careful.

JAN. Where were you?

MARYSIA. At church.

JAN. By yourself?

MARYSIA. By myself.

JAN. And not with my only-begotten son?

MARYSIA. Fuck your only-begotten son.

JAN. That's precisely what I'm afraid of. Sometimes people say
things to you so seriously that you think they're lying. Or you
hope they are. Do you want a bit of cake? I left it for you.

MARYSIA. Leave it for him.

JAN. He's too fat. When I was his age, I didn't eat anything.
I've worked hard all my life and what's my reward?
Backache.

MARYSIA. Come here, I'll give you a massage. You're a
workaholic. One day off and you're already in pain.

JAN. I don't want a massage. You two think you can just go off
and leave old Dad here alone in front of the barbecue. May I
remind you in what capacity you're here? That's no way for
an assistant to behave.

MARYSIA. I'm your slave. I'd rather hear one of your 'fuck
off's than a thousand of his 'hello, how are you, it's
awesome, brilliant, amazing, exciting'. And that's the truth.

JAN. Then why do you never reply to my text messages? I think
you're a real piece of shit for not replying.

MARYSIA. I don't even know what to write in my texts any
more. 'Hello M, are you missing me?' And that stupid
fucking emoticon you put in every fucking text with the big
smiley face. What do you want me to say to that? I think
you're a real piece of shit for existing.

JAN. If I text you, I expect an answer. Especially if the message
ends with a question mark.

MARYSIA. I think you should be more worried about actual
problems. Like your bank balance. Anti-Ageing Exfoliation
Mask – five hundred złoty, Activate Eye Gel – seven hundred
złoty, Professional Man Face Serum – three hundred złoty?

JAN. And I think your mum should be more worried about her
daughter the eternal virgin, who came to me on her knees
begging me to kill her child.

MARYSIA. Keep talking. Kick me. Throw your cigarette ends at me. Spit on me, just so you make yourself absolutely clear.

JAN. Even my über-tolerant son thinks that prevention is better than cure.

MARYSIA. You told him.

JAN. Of course I did. I warned him that you, young lady, are a witch. This is killing me. I have feelings too, you know. (*Beat.*) I'm sorry. Honestly.

MARYSIA. Where are your feelings?

JAN. A bit of affection and everything would be easier. If you were just a little nicer to me... You're nice to Piotr. I don't see why you can't be nice to me.

MARYSIA. Piotr's a total dickhead, Daddy. It's about time you realised that!

JAN. Well, who isn't? Have a drink. Everything's easier once you've had a drink.

MARYSIA. Anyone would think you were about to die. Slow down a bit!

JAN. Have a drink.

MARYSIA. I'm not drinking.

JAN. You're not drinking because you...

MARYSIA. I'm just not.

JAN. I see. Are you not feeling well?

MARYSIA. I feel fine. Why?

JAN. Why? I don't know. But I'll tell you why nothing's fine. It's because you've got nothing to live for.

MARYSIA. Well, have you given me anything to live for?

JAN. What would you want?

MARYSIA. I don't know.

JAN. You live near me and I can tell you now that that's better than living with me, if that's what you're driving at. Anyway, you always manage to leave greasy fingerprints over everything. You're always losing things or stealing things. Leaving your snotty tissues lying on the table. How can you live like that? I can't sleep if the place is that messy.

MARYSIA. So that's why you're happy to pay two lots of rent?

JAN. That's right.

MARYSIA. I was thinking. Whilst we're here, you could go and visit the woman who still has the legal right to call herself your wife and tell her –

JAN. Legal rights mean nothing in this country.

MARYSIA. Is she the one who doesn't want to get divorced? Is it against her beliefs? Or is it you who doesn't want to? Sometimes I'm not sure.

JAN. Wives just happen to a man sometimes. I'm not going to apologise to you for that.

MARYSIA. Divorce is a sin. There's no place for it in God's plans, but if you found a place for it in our human plans, I'd be happier. It would be a sign, wouldn't it? So why don't you go and talk to her?

JAN. I'm forbidden fruit, but you're still with me. I don't force you to stay, do I? Have a think about that. You know, you still haven't told me how your holiday was. What did you see? Did you like Big Ben?

MARYSIA. It was so small I didn't even notice it. I walked straight past it. It looks better on postcards.

JAN. What did you do? How did you do it?

MARYSIA. We shagged hanging off a chandelier in Westminster Cathedral. What else do you want to know? Why did you even let me go?

JAN. Why did you agree? Why didn't you come back sooner? I asked you to. It was humiliating. And you didn't even bother to reply.

MARYSIA. I wanted to. But at the same time – I didn't. I love you, but I don't like you.

JAN. And do you like him? When you talk to him, the tone of your voice changes. It drops half an octave. It sounds sort of oiled. You can't stop yourself.

MARYSIA. I wish –

JAN. Yes?

MARYSIA. That it was you and me who were –

JAN. What?

MARYSIA. Nothing. When a sin takes place, everything changes. Is it nice having a child? What's it like?

JAN. Hassle. Hassle and boredom. Have a good long think before you decide to have any. You're not naive enough to believe all those fairytales about how wonderful it is, are you?

MARYSIA. Would you like to have a baby with me?

JAN. I'm too old for all that.

MARYSIA. Why does every festival have to end with a hangover and a mess and everything in ruins? I need a drink.

Scene Thirteen

15th August 2010. Midnight. Niepokalanów. Outside the church.

ALL. Happy birthday to you, happy birthday to you…

PIOTR. Does anyone fancy a beer?

MARYSIA. I wouldn't say no. (*To* JAN.) And could you add just the tiniest splash of vodka?

JAN. Certainly. Here you go.

MARYSIA. Excuse me, would you mind awfully if I took one of your cigarettes?

PIOTR. Not in the slightest.

MARYSIA. Thank you. These are just wonderful.

JAN. Why aren't you eating the cake? Don't you like it any more?

MARYSIA. It's delicious, but I can't eat another thing. I need to have a clear head today. And the best way of achieving that is by drinking heavily.

PIOTR. Alcohol can be harmful to health. Did you ever buy that cat you wanted?

MARYSIA. I got one, but it drowned itself in the river. I think it realised that I'd never be able to look after it.

JAN. I might go to church.

MARYSIA. There's no point, it's cold inside. Besides, God's taken the day off like everyone else.

PIOTR. I still haven't got my present.

JAN. I ordered a chandelier from Westminster Cathedral for you. It's in the post.

PIOTR. I feel sick.

MARYSIA. Too much cake, I told you so. You should drink raspberry juice. You'll miss the last train. Laters! Will you drink a London Cosmopolitan for me?

PIOTR. Of course.

MARYSIA. And one for the cat. Please.

   PIOTR *exits.*

JAN. Is it his?

MARYSIA. I think you should go now.

JAN. Why?

MARYSIA. Because I want to be my own therapist for a while. Go on. Go and check the car tyres. Go. Go.

   JAN *exits.*

   The bell strikes midnight. The Taboo cards lie scattered across the stage.

   (*To the audience.*) My child would be naughty, mean and unhappy.

   I would twist its ear if it didn't shut up.

   I would rap its knuckles for not listening to me.

   Tell it to go to sleep and not get up for a month.

   Stick tape over its mouth to stop it crying.

   I wouldn't be able to change its nappy.

   I wouldn't be able to wash it.

   I'd be scared it would fall out of my arms.

   I'd cry if I had to leave it alone.

   It would grow and I'd stop liking it, because I only like little things, kittens and puppies, and when they get bigger I want to get rid of them.

   There's no going back. Man up, woman. Do the right thing.

Love is not what you feel, it's what you decide to do. That's how it is sometimes. You wake up and you know: this has to stop, this has to stop, this has to stop.

Hail Mary, full of grace, the Lord is with thee. Blessed art thou among women and blessed is the fruit of thy womb, Jesus. Holy Mary Mother of God, pray for us sinners now and at the hour of our death.

Hail Mary, full of God, I am with thee. Cursed art thou among women and cursed is the fruit of thy womb, nothing. Holy Mary, lonely Mary, pray for us sinners. At the hour of our death.

Hail Mary. Full of drink. No one is with thee. Pray for… Us. Now. Blessed is nothing. Pray for us among women. The hour of our deaths. The fruit of thy womb. Fruit of thy womb. Mother. Mother. Mother. Grace. Grace. Grace.

Scene Fourteen – Epilogue

JAN. I lost her. I waited for her. I knew she wouldn't come back. Back in Warsaw, I find two of her hairs on my desk. I blow them away.

PIOTR. That hangover is different to any hangover I've ever had before. It cleanses me. I never call her. I block her on Facebook. I go home. I get the cheapest flight I can find. Wizz Air.

JAN. Everything's all right after that. I'll live until I'm eighty. I'll be healthy. I'll visit my son in the UK four times. That's enough. Each time I'll have to send him a card when I get back: 'So sorry, I forgot your present again! I'll bring it next time!' When I'm sixty, I'll start taking pills for my blood pressure and some Valium just in case. I'll die alone. Heart attack. Job title: professional. Eyes: blue. Children: one. Religion: human being.

PIOTR. Everything's fine. I'll live fast and unhealthily and smoke like a chimney until my ulcer bursts on my thirty-fifth birthday. In hospital I'll meet Scarlett. She's beautiful and I'll fall in love with her, because she reminds me of Scarlett Johansson and who wouldn't fall in love with Scarlett Johansson? Job title: director of a TV law show. Eyes: blue. Children: three – Will, Tadeus and John.

MARYSIA. It's all going to be okay. I'll lead a quiet life. I'll die of some form of cancer, something in my abdomen – because if you don't have physical contact with another person or an animal three times a day, you get cancer. But until then – my heart has to keep beating. Job title: school nurse, back in Niepokalanów. Eyes: brown. Children: none.

A Nick Hern Book

A Time to Reap first published in Great Britain as a paperback original in
2013 by Nick Hern Books Limited, The Glasshouse, 49a Goldhawk Road,
London W12 8QP, in association with the Royal Court Theatre, London

Cover image: Matt Herring
Cover design: Ned Hoste, 2H

Typeset by Nick Hern Books, London
Printed and bound in Great Britain by CPI Group (UK) Ltd

A CIP catalogue record for this book is available from the British Library

ISBN 978 1 84842 324 4